Afternoon Tea
at
Pittock Mansion
Recipes & Reminiscences

The Pittock Mansion Society

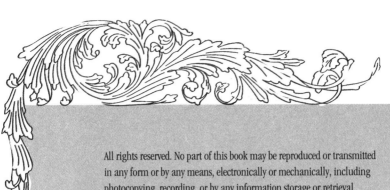

Cover illustration: Janora Bayot
Text illustrations: Sueanne Townley
Graphic Design and Typography: Design Studio Selby
Back Cover photograph: Michael Henley, Contemporary Images

Copyright © 2003 by the Pittock Mansion Society
Printed in the United States of America.
ISBN 1-892347-02-4

Published by: The Pittock Mansion Society
3229 NW Pittock Drive
Portland, OR 97210
(503) 823-3625

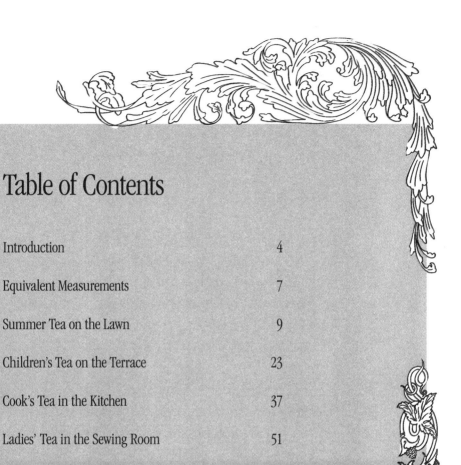

Table of Contents

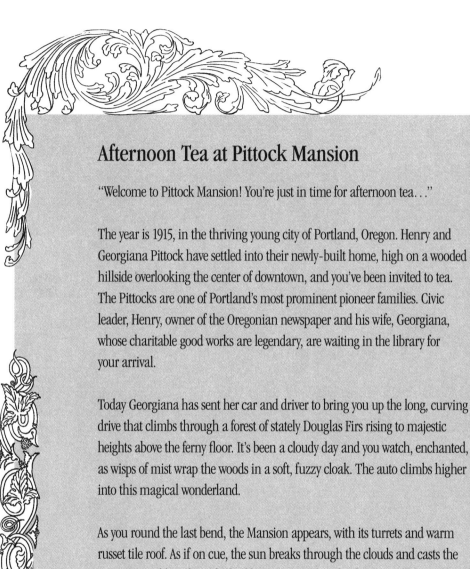

Afternoon Tea at Pittock Mansion

"Welcome to Pittock Mansion! You're just in time for afternoon tea…"

The year is 1915, in the thriving young city of Portland, Oregon. Henry and Georgiana Pittock have settled into their newly-built home, high on a wooded hillside overlooking the center of downtown, and you've been invited to tea. The Pittocks are one of Portland's most prominent pioneer families. Civic leader, Henry, owner of the Oregonian newspaper and his wife, Georgiana, whose charitable good works are legendary, are waiting in the library for your arrival.

Today Georgiana has sent her car and driver to bring you up the long, curving drive that climbs through a forest of stately Douglas Firs rising to majestic heights above the ferny floor. It's been a cloudy day and you watch, enchanted, as wisps of mist wrap the woods in a soft, fuzzy cloak. The auto climbs higher into this magical wonderland.

As you round the last bend, the Mansion appears, with its turrets and warm russet tile roof. As if on cue, the sun breaks through the clouds and casts the scene in a golden glow. If it had been a rainy day, the driver would have driven to the porte cochère entrance, where the protective cover would keep you dry. Since the sun is shining, he stops at the Mansion's front door, with its intricate ironwork.

On other occasions a maid might escort you up the magnificent curved marble staircase to the Sewing Room, where Mrs. Pittock and the ladies are at work making baby clothing for one of their favorite charities.

Or perhaps tea will be served in the oval Music Room, with daughters Kate and Lucy entertaining the guests with vocal and piano harmony.

If the season is summer and the day is warm, plans might include a picnic tea on the lawn, while the grandchildren romp on the terrace.

There are so many Pittock Mansion tea "adventures" to be enjoyed in the pages of this book, from *High Tea in the Dining Room* to *Cook's Tea in the Kitchen*; from a *Fundraising Tea* for one of Mrs. Pittock's favorite charities, to *Christmas Tea in the Library*. Through recipes and treasured family photographs, you're invited to enjoy tea as it might have been served in 1915, when Henry and Georgiana Pittock hosted family get-togethers and elegant gatherings at Pittock Mansion.

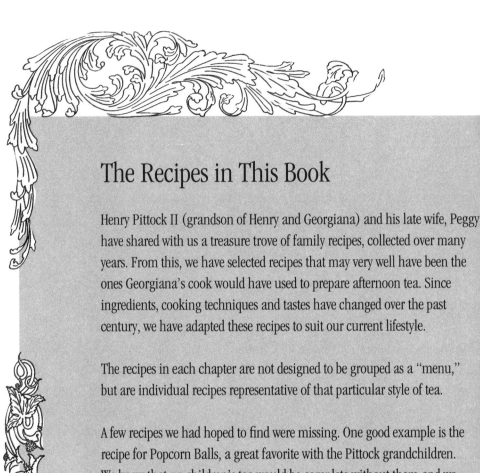

The Recipes in This Book

Henry Pittock II (grandson of Henry and Georgiana) and his late wife, Peggy have shared with us a treasure trove of family recipes, collected over many years. From this, we have selected recipes that may very well have been the ones Georgiana's cook would have used to prepare afternoon tea. Since ingredients, cooking techniques and tastes have changed over the past century, we have adapted these recipes to suit our current lifestyle.

The recipes in each chapter are not designed to be grouped as a "menu," but are individual recipes representative of that particular style of tea.

A few recipes we had hoped to find were missing. One good example is the recipe for Popcorn Balls, a great favorite with the Pittock grandchildren. We knew that no children's tea would be complete without them and we even have the photographs to prove it! Yet there was no mention of a Popcorn Ball in the vast compendium of Pittock recipes. A serious oversight! In the few cases like these, we have taken the liberty to develop a recipe that v feel would be representative of the era.

We hope that you'll enjoy the pleasures of *Afternoon Tea at Pittock Mansior*

Equivalent Measurements

A dash = 2 to 4 drops

3 teaspoons = 1 Tablespoon

4 Tablespoons = 1/4 cup

16 Tablespoons = 1 cup

4 cups = 1 quart

Metric Equivalents

Liquid Volume:

1/4 teaspoon = 1 milliliter

1/2 teaspoon = 2 milliliters

1 teaspoon = 5 milliliters

1 Tablespoon = 15 milliliters

1/4 cup = 60 milliliters

1/3 cup = 75 milliliters

1/2 cup = 118 milliliters

2/3 cup = 150 milliliters

3/4 cup = 178 milliliters

1 cup = 240 milliliters

Dry Weight:

1 ounce = 30 grams

2 ounces = 59 grams

3 ounces = 85 grams

4 ounces = 118 grams

5 ounces = 140 grams

6 ounces = 178 grams

7 ounces = 200 grams

8 ounces = 240 grams

10 ounces = 480 grams

Oven Temperatures:

350° F = 180° C

375° F = 190° C.

400° F = 200° C

425° F = 220° C

450° F = 230° C

This is one of the hushed, ripe days
when we fancy we might hear the
beating of nature's heart.

John Muir

Summer Tea on the Lawn

It's a hot summer day on the city streets of Portland, but high on the hill at the Pittocks' home, a soft breeze keeps the temperature just right for an *al fresco* tea. With the scent of Georgiana's favorite roses and the irresistible goodies arrayed on the starched linen cloth, the Pittocks are ready to enjoy the pleasures of a summer afternoon.

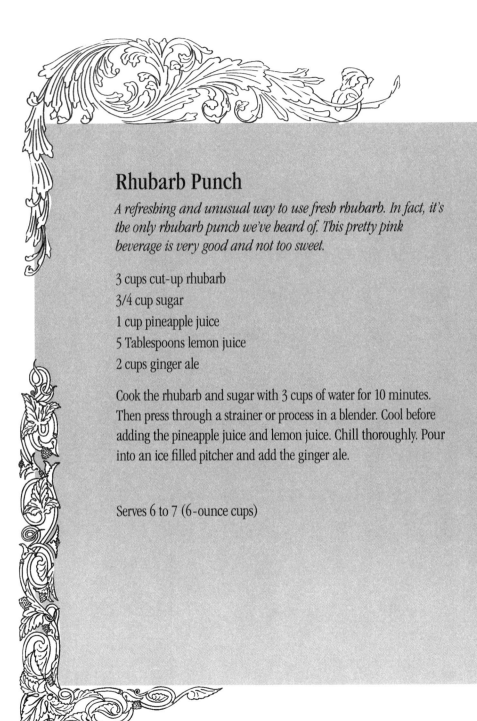

Rhubarb Punch

A refreshing and unusual way to use fresh rhubarb. In fact, it's the only rhubarb punch we've heard of. This pretty pink beverage is very good and not too sweet.

3 cups cut-up rhubarb
3/4 cup sugar
1 cup pineapple juice
5 Tablespoons lemon juice
2 cups ginger ale

Cook the rhubarb and sugar with 3 cups of water for 10 minutes. Then press through a strainer or process in a blender. Cool before adding the pineapple juice and lemon juice. Chill thoroughly. Pour into an ice filled pitcher and add the ginger ale.

Serves 6 to 7 (6-ounce cups)

n this happy family photo, c.1912, the Pittocks, Leadbetters and Gantenbeins,
Henry and Georgiana's offspring, enjoyed an outing in a ferny glen. Henry Pittock
s the diminutive gentleman standing second from the right in the front row.

In this old photograph of an outing in the woods, young Henry Pittock
center. The flag suggests that this was a patriotic occasion, perhaps
the Fourth of July.

Peggy's Wedding Cake Cookies

Peggy Pittock, wife of Henry Pittock II, gathered a collection of family recipes that inspired this book. This recipe, for a melt-in-your-mouth cookie, is one of her own.

1 cup softened butter
1/2 cup powdered sugar
1 teaspoon vanilla
2 cups flour
1/4 teaspoon salt
Additional powdered sugar for coating

Preheat oven to 375° F. With an electric mixer, cream the butter well. Gradually add the sugar and beat until light and fluffy. Gradually add flour, vanilla and salt. Beat at low speed until well blended.

Pinch off pieces of dough and roll with hands into 1-inch balls or finger shapes. Roll cookies in powdered sugar. If too soft to handle, chill dough about 15 minutes before shaping. Place on cookie sheet and bake 10 minutes.

Makes about 4 dozen cookies

Angel Whispers

This is a pretty, rather unusual cookie, just lovely served at a tea. Love the name! And you'll love the cookie!!

1 cup butter or margarine
1/2 cup sifted confectioner's sugar
1 teaspoon lemon extract
2 cups sifted flour
1/4 teaspoon salt

Preheat oven to 350° F. In a large mixing bowl, cream butter or margarine to the consistency of mayonnaise. Add sugar gradually and continue to cream. Add remaining ingredients and blend well. Chill until firm, about one hour.

Measure one level teaspoon of dough. Form into ball and flatten slightly. Place about 1 inch apart on ungreased baking sheet. Bake for 8 to 10 minutes or until edges are lightly browned. Put together with lemon filling.

Lemon Filling:

1 egg, slightly beaten
3 Tablespoons lemon juice
Grated peel of 1 lemon
2/3 cup sugar
1 1/2 Tablespoons softened margarine

Blend all ingredients in top of double boiler. Cook over hot water, stirring constantly, until thick. Chill until firm.

The Pittocks enjoyed outdoor life. Shown here on a berry-picking excursion at the oast are Henry Pittock and his wife Georgiana (kneeling in back).

Spicy Blueberry Tea Cake

A nice change from muffins—a true tea cake,
and anything with blueberries is the best!

1/2 cup butter or margarine

1 cup sugar

2 eggs

2 cups flour, sifted

2 Tablespoons baking powder

1 teaspoon cinnamon

1 teaspoon grated orange peel

1/2 teaspoon salt

1/2 teaspoon ground cloves

1 cup blueberries, fresh or frozen (if using frozen, drain well)

1/2 cup orange juice

1 teaspoon vanilla

Sift together flour, baking powder, cinnamon, cloves, and salt. Cream butter or margarine with sugar. Add eggs and blend until fluffy. Add vanilla and grated orange peel. Mix a small amount of the flour mixture with the blueberries—set aside. Add flour mixture alternately with the orange juice, beating well after each addition. Fold in the blueberries. Bake in greased and floured Bundt pan at 350° F for about 40 minutes. Cool in pan on rack for 10 minutes.

Remove from pan and drizzle with Orange Glaze.

Orange Glaze:

1 cup powdered sugar
2 to 3 Tablespoons orange juice

Blend orange juice into powdered sugar until the desired consistency to drizzle over cake.

Serves 10

Tester's Note: This is not a very large cake. It looks pretty made in a Bundt pan but is only about 2 inches tall. A good tea cake size.

For a Pittock picnic, sweets were essential and cakes were a popular favorite. Daughter Kate Leadbetter can be seen seated at left, and Lucy at right, while Her Pittock, behind the group on the right, appears ready for another piece of cake. Pittock, Henry and Georgiana's son, was such a coffee lover that he'd bring his o pot for a fresh brew. Musical instruments were brought to brighten the occasion.

Orange Pound Cake

The Pittocks loved to picnic and in most of the old picnic photos, you'll see at least one cake box. Orange Pound Cake was a Pittock favorite.

1/2 cup butter
2 1/2 cups sugar
4 eggs
3 cups flour
1/2 teaspoon baking soda
3/4 cup buttermilk
1/4 cup Cointreau or other orange-flavored liqueur
1 Tablespoon grated orange peel
1 teaspoon vanilla

Cream butter and sugar together. Add 4 eggs. Sift the flour and baking soda together. Blend the buttermilk with the liqueur, orange peel and vanilla. Combine all ingredients and pour batter into greased and floured tube pan or Bundt pan. Bake at 350° F for about 1 hour. Cool cake in pan 10 minutes. Turn out onto a rack to cool.

Serves 10 to 12

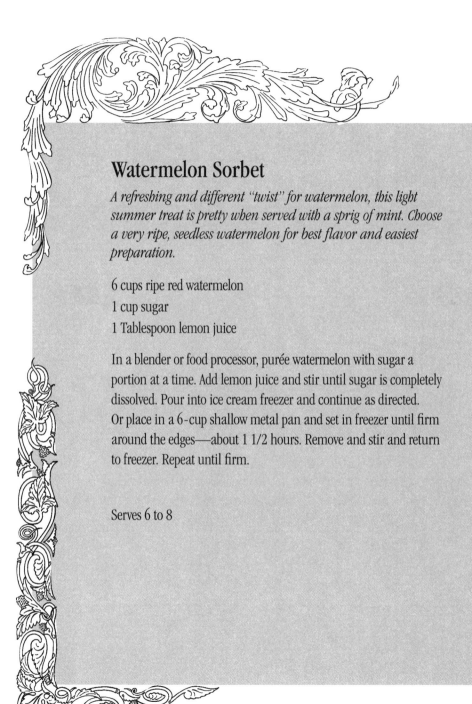

Watermelon Sorbet

A refreshing and different "twist" for watermelon, this light summer treat is pretty when served with a sprig of mint. Choose a very ripe, seedless watermelon for best flavor and easiest preparation.

6 cups ripe red watermelon
1 cup sugar
1 Tablespoon lemon juice

In a blender or food processor, purée watermelon with sugar a portion at a time. Add lemon juice and stir until sugar is completely dissolved. Pour into ice cream freezer and continue as directed. Or place in a 6-cup shallow metal pan and set in freezer until firm around the edges—about 1 1/2 hours. Remove and stir and return to freezer. Repeat until firm.

Serves 6 to 8

Candied Rose Petals

Georgiana's favorite flowers were roses and we love this way of preserving them. They're elegant and so lovely in a pretty dish or as decoration on a cake.

2 to 3 cups rose petals (from unsprayed roses)
1 egg white (*see Note below)
1 Tablespoon cold water
Sugar for dipping

Beat 1 egg white with 1 Tablespoon cold water. Using a pastry brush, brush the mixture on both sides of a rose petal. Dip in a shallow bowl of granulated sugar, dry on a wire rack. Store between paper towels in an airtight container, up to 2 months.

*Note: Uncooked egg whites can harbor salmonella. To be perfectly safe, you may choose to buy "pasteurized" eggs, sold at several local stores. These are whole eggs that have been heated gently to eliminate the possibility of salmonella. Another option is to use powdered egg whites as a substitute.

It was spring on the terrace
that bright day in May
With Rhoda and Teddy and me.
Cook baked us treats that were
tiny sweet bites
And let us use china for tea.

Bramble Burns

Children's Tea on the Terrace

The Pittock grandchildren, some of whom had the good fortune to live at the Mansion, loved to play in all the nooks and crannies of the house and to explore the forty-six acres of woods and gardens. At play time, after a day at school, they'd have great fun calling downstairs on the intercom to request cookies, which the cook willingly sent up to them on the dumbwaiter. Into their adulthood, the children fondly remembered the special treats made by the Pittock cooks.

Crab Burgers

A delicious way to serve Northwest crabmeat and a nice change from "regular" burgers.

2 cups crab meat
3 hard cooked eggs, chopped
1/4 cup chopped ripe olives
1/2 cup mayonnaise
1/2 cup chili or seafood sauce
Juice of 1/2 lemon
6 hamburger buns
1 cup grated cheese

Combine crabmeat with chopped eggs and olives. In a separate bowl combine mayonnaise, chili sauce, and lemon juice. Add to crab mixture and blend. (Mix should be moist.) Spread on bottom half of split hamburger buns. Sprinkle with grated cheese. Broil until cheese melts and burger is heated. Serve with top of bun.

Serves 6

Tester's Notes: Crab burgers were a pleasant surprise. Very easy to make and made 6 generous burgers. This would be great to serve on a warm summer day, after a morning of crabbing at the beach.

randdaughters Georgiana Gantenbein (at left) and her cousin, Fredrika Pittock,
ayed near the porte cochère in this charming 1917 photograph.

One summer day, around 1920, cousins Peter Gantenbein (at left) and Henry Pittock II, paused their playing long enough for this delightful photograph to be snapped.

Orange Cupcakes

*An unusual recipe—and an unusually good one at that
—for a cupcake that needs no extra frosting.*

1/2 cup butter
1 cup sugar
2 eggs, beaten
1 cup sour cream
2 cups flour
1 teaspoon baking soda
1 cup raisins
Rind of 2 oranges
1 1/2 cups orange juice
1 1/2 cups sugar

Grease and flour muffin pans. Cream butter and add sugar. Add
eggs and sour cream alternately with sifted flour and baking soda.
Add raisins and orange peel. Spoon mixture into pans. Bake in
350° F oven for 25 to 30 minutes. Remove from oven. Mix orange
juice and sugar and pour over hot cupcakes. Let cool and remove
from pans.

Makes 24 to 30 good-sized cupcakes

Popcorn Balls

No Pittock cookbook would be complete without popcorn balls—a Pittock favorite! This recipe makes about 2 dozen small or 18 medium balls.

20 cups popped corn (1 cup unpopped or about 3 microwave bags)
2 cups sugar
1 1/2 cups water
1/2 cup light corn syrup
1 teaspoon vinegar
1/2 teaspoon salt
1 teaspoon vanilla
Butter

Make the popcorn and keep it warm in an oven at very low heat, about 250° F. Lightly butter or oil a large, heavy saucepan and a scoop (to be used later to shape the popcorn balls). Combine sugar, water, corn syrup, vinegar, and salt in the saucepan, stirring until sugar is dissolved. Cook over medium heat without stirring, until the mixture reaches the hard crack stage (270° F on a candy thermometer).

Remove from heat, stir in the vanilla and immediately pour over the warm popcorn, mixing well. Using buttered hands and scoop, quickly form into balls and set aside to cool.

The Pittock grandchildren loved the popcorn balls made for them by Cook. In this c.1918 photograph, nine grandchildren enjoy one of their favorite treats: (*back row, left to right*) Rhoda Gantenbein, with Roberta, Barbara, Marjorie and Virginia Pittock; (*front row, left to right*) Henry Pittock II, Peter and Georgiana Gantenbein, Fredrika Pittock.

Georgiana, a doting grandmother, is shown in this photograph (c.1910) cuddling two of the Pittock grandchildren, at *Lakeside*, the home of Fred Pittock at Lacamas Lake, Washington.

Emma's Hermits

2/3 cup butter

1 cup brown sugar

2 eggs

1/4 teaspoon baking soda

2 Tablespoons sour cream, milk or buttermilk

2 teaspoons cinnamon

1/2 teaspoon nutmeg

1/4 teaspoon ground cloves

1/4 teaspoon ground ginger

1 3/4 cups sifted flour

1 cup chopped nuts

1/2 cup chopped raisins

1/2 cup chopped citron, prunes or dates

Glaze:

3/4 cup powdered sugar

1 teaspoon or more lemon juice

Preheat oven to 350°F. In a large mixing bowl, cream butter and sugar. Add eggs, mixing well. In a measuring cup or small bowl, dissolve the baking soda in the cream. Add spices to the butter mixture, mixing well. Add flour and liquids, alternately, about a third at a time, stirring until well blended. Fold in nuts, raisins and citron, prunes or dates.

Drop by rounded teaspoonfuls onto greased and floured cookie sheets. Bake for 12 to 15 minutes until golden brown. **Glaze:** In a small bowl, combine powered sugar and lemon juice. Brush tops of cookies when cooled.

Makes 2 dozen

Berry Good Ice Cream

The fresh taste of summer in Oregon! This recipe gives two different ways to make this treat—in an ice cream machine or in your own freezer.

2 cups fresh berries
1 1/2 cups sugar
2 cups heavy cream
2 cups half and half
2 teaspoons vanilla
Pinch of salt

Mash berries with sugar. Let stand at room temperature for one hour. Combine with remaining ingredients. Chill in refrigerator for one hour or more. Churn in an ice cream machine according to instructions until firm. You may also place in freezer, stirring every hour as mixture becomes firm.

Makes about 1 1/2 quarts

At play in a wagon on the Mansion grounds circa 1918 are: (*standing at left*) Fredrika Pittock, (*in wagon, back to front*) Barbara Pittock, Rhoda Gantenbein and Peter Gantenbein peeking out behind Henry Pittock II. Standing at right is Roberta Pittock.

Crispy Oatmeal Cookies

Classic perfection in an oatmeal cookie, this recipe's a winner!

1 cup butter or margarine

1 cup white sugar

1 cup brown sugar

2 eggs

1 teaspoon vanilla

1 1/2 cups sifted flour

1/2 teaspoon salt

1/2 teaspoon soda

3 cups regular rolled oats

3/4 cup chopped walnuts

Combine flour, salt, soda, and oats. Set aside. Cream butter and sugars until fluffy. Add eggs one at time, mixing after each addition. Blend in vanilla. Stir in flour mixture, mixing well. Add walnuts. Chill dough for at least one hour. Shape into one inch balls. Place on greased cookie sheet. Then flatten with a glass dipped in sugar. Bake at 350° F for 12 to 14 minutes or until lightly browned.

Variation:

Coconut Oatmeal: Decrease oatmeal to 2 cups, add 1 cup coconut and use 3/4 cup chopped pecans instead of walnuts.

Makes 5 dozen

Tester's Notes: This is a very good cookie. I made a variation with some chocolate chips for my chocoholic husband and those were also very good.

Brownie Pudding Cake

Very rich, moist and yummy!
It also tastes delicious served with whipped cream.

Cake:

1 cup flour
3/4 cup sugar
2 Tablespoons cocoa
2 teaspoons baking powder
1/2 teaspoon salt
1/2 cup milk
2 Tablespoons oil
1 teaspoon vanilla
1 3/4 cups hot water

Topping:

3/4 cup brown sugar
1/4 cup cocoa

Sift together dry cake ingredients. To this mixture, add the milk, salad oil, and vanilla. Place this mixture in a greased square baking pan. Mix brown sugar, 1/4 cup cocoa and sprinkle over batter. Pour 1 3/4 cups hot water over all. Bake in a 350° F oven for 35 to 40 minutes.

Serves 6 to 8

Cook, Cook, drink your tea,
But save some in the pot for me.
We'll watch the tea leaves in our cup
When our drink is all sipped up.
Happiness or fortune great,
What will our future be?

R. Z. Berry

Cook's Tea in the Kitchen

The Pittock kitchen was a marvel of up-to-date kitchen design, with all of the latest equipment to thrill the heart of any cook.

At teatime, the servants would gather there for a meal that was "homey" and substantial enough to give them energy to finish the day. It may not be what we would consider "afternoon tea," with fine china and fussy goodies, but was comprised of plain food, beautifully prepared.

Chinese Chicken Mushroom Soup

What do you eat when you have a Chinese cook and a chicken farm?
The family enjoyed plenty of chicken from one of Henry's investments,
a chicken farm. Here is a recipe in honor of one of their cooks,
who was indeed Chinese.

1/2 pound boneless, skinless chicken breast (1 large half)

1 teaspoon salt, divided

1 tablespoon cornstarch

3 tablespoons cold water

1 Tablespoon soy sauce

4 cups chicken broth or bouillon or stock

6 fresh mushrooms, sliced or 4-ounce can sliced mushrooms

1 1/2 Tablespoons cooking oil

2 Tablespoons lemon juice

3/4 cup cooked white rice, optional

Thin lemon slices

Slice chicken into 10 pieces. Sprinkle with 1/2 teaspoon salt and let stand 30 minutes. Mix cornstarch with cold water. Add corn starch mixture and remaining salt and soy sauce to stock. Bring to a boil. Lower heat and simmer chicken in this for 5 minutes. Sauté mushrooms in oil a few minutes. Add mushrooms to chicken broth; adjust salt if necessary. Heat gently without boiling. Serve with a thin lemon slice in each bowl.

5 servings

Tester's note: A nice, serve-again, soup.

The view from the kitchen window is a majestic panorama of
mountains, river and trees, with the city of Portland far below.

The Pittock Mansion greenhouse no longer is standing, but this old photograph reminds us that many of the fresh fruits and vegetables served at meals were grown right on the mansion grounds.

Fresh Tomato Soup

Henry had a greenhouse where he grew fresh tomatoes.
This is a wonderful way to use them when the garden has been
a bit too bountiful.

4 cups crushed tomatoes (may use canned tomatoes, if necessary)
2 cups tomato juice
2 cups chicken broth
12 to 14 fresh basil leaves
1 cup whipping cream
1 stick sweet butter
Salt and pepper to taste

Combine tomatoes, juice and broth. Simmer for 30 minutes.
Purée, along with basil. Return to pan. Add cream and butter,
while stirring, over low heat.

Serves 4 to 6

Henry's Shirred Eggs With Ham

A particular favorite with Henry Pittock II, as made by his mother, Bertha Leadbetter Pittock for her only son.

1 1/2 cups chopped, cooked ham
1/4 cup grated Parmesan cheese
6 eggs

Sauce:
2 Tablespoons butter
2 Tablespoons flour
1/8 teaspoon salt
1 cup milk
2 tablespoons Parmesan cheese

3 toasted English muffins, split

Preheat oven to 350° F. Grease 6 custard cups with butter or oil. Combine ham and 1/4 cup of cheese. Break an egg in each custard cup. Top each with 1/4 cup of ham and cheese mixture. Put cups in a large baking dish; pour in hot water to 1-inch depth. Bake at 350° F for 25 minutes.

Make sauce: Melt butter, stir in flour and salt. Remove from heat, add milk. Cook over medium heat, stirring till thick. Cook two more minutes. Stir in 2 Tablespoons of Parmesan cheese.

To serve: Invert an egg on each muffin half and top with cheese sauce.

Makes 6 servings

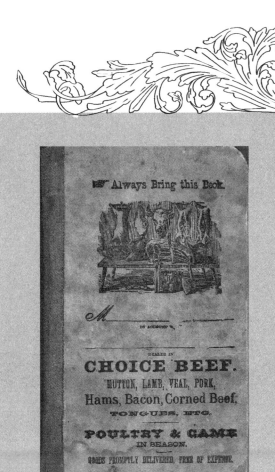

$\mathcal{M}$

IN ACCOUNT W.

DEALER IN

CHOICE BEEF.
MUTTON, LAMB, VEAL, PORK,
Hams, Bacon, Corned Beef,
TONGUES, ETC.

POULTRY & GAME
IN SEASON.

GOODS PROMPTLY DELIVERED, FREE OF EXPENSE.

We're fortunate to have one of the original Pittock kitchen account books from July 1889, where Cook would keep track of food purchases. Its pages tell of "beef steak - 25 cents", "milk - 10 cents" and "cauliflower - 15 cents." It also gives us a clear inventory of the kitchen utensils and equipment used, including "1 mush boiler", "1 pie board", and "3 tin dippers".

The magnificent range, built in 1913-14, is the focal point in today's restored Pittock kitchen. Cook is making a batch of Oatmeal Pancakes for the servant's hearty tea.

Oatmeal Pancakes

Delicate and delicious pancakes that are flavored with cinnamon and dotted with raisins.

This batter must be started the night before. Combine the following two ingredients. Stir to blend well, cover and refrigerate all night.

2 cups rolled oats

2 cups buttermilk

In the morning, add the eggs, butter and raisins. Stir just to blend.

2 eggs, lightly beaten

1/4 cup butter melted and cooled

1/2 cup raisins

In another bowl combine the following ingredients:

1/2 cup flour (whole wheat flour may be used)

2 tablespoons sugar

1 teaspoon each baking powder and soda

1/2 teaspoon cinnamon

1/2 teaspoon salt

Add to oat mixture and stir until just moistened; if batter seems too thick, stir in up to 4 to 5 tablespoons buttermilk. Use about 1/4 cup batter for each cake. Cook on a lightly greased or Teflon griddle. Cook on a lower heat than other pancakes so they will cook in the middle.

Makes about 15 pancakes

Tester's note: These are really great tasty pancakes and worth the effort.

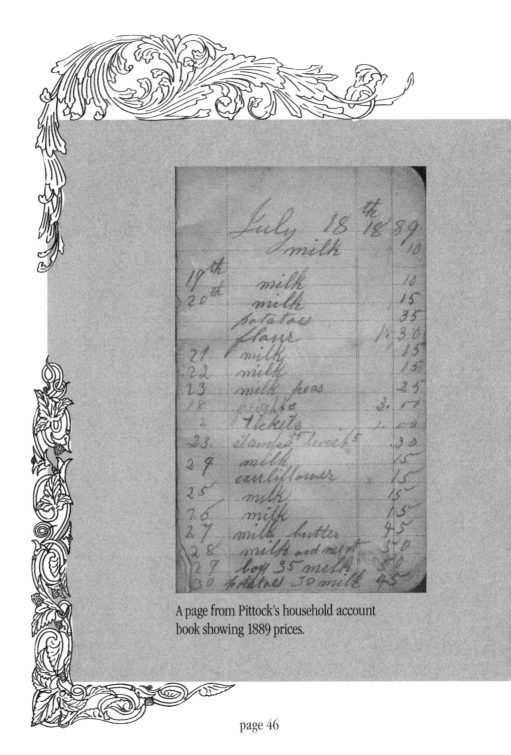

A page from Pittock's household account
book showing 1889 prices.

Stuffed and Baked Fish

This recipe works well as either a whole stuffed fish or two fillets with stuffing between.

2 cups bread crumbs
1 small onion, chopped
3 slices bacon, divided, 2 whole and 1 chopped
2 Tablespoons green pepper, chopped
1/2 teaspoon pepper
1/2 teaspoon salt
1/4 teaspoon savory
3 pounds fish with firm white flesh

Split dressed fish and spread with the above mixture. Fold fish over the bottom half and close with skewers. Place fish on baking rack in a baking pan. Lay 2 slices of bacon on top of fish. Bake in a covered dish at 450° F for 20 or 30 minutes.

Serves 6

Tester's note: A very good recipe. Served with brown rice and salad, it makes a great meal.

Date Pudding and Cookies

This versatile "either/or" recipe can be either a pudding or cookies. Your choice!

2 eggs
3/4 cup sugar
2 Tablespoons flour
1 teaspoon baking powder
1/2 teaspoon salt
1 cup pecans, chopped
1 cup dates, chopped

Preheat oven to 350° F. Grease an 8-inch square cake pan. In a large mixing bowl, beat eggs. Stir in sugar. Combine flour, baking powder and salt. Add to egg mixture, beating well. Fold in nuts and dates. Pour into prepared pan. Bake for 30 to 40 minutes. Cut into squares and serve warm with whipped cream.

Serves 8

Variation: Date Cookies

Follow the directions above to mix and bake the pudding. After baking, remove the pan from the oven. Let cool a little. While pudding is still warm, but not hot, remove teaspoonfuls of pudding and roll into walnut sized balls. Then roll the balls in powdered sugar.

Tester's Notes: Very unusual. I don't think I've ever seen a recipe that could be either a pudding or cookies, but delicious either way.

Mapril's Apple Crisp

Peggy Pittock borrowed this recipe from her mother, Mapril Keasey, and we're glad she didn't return it! Very yummy.

8 baking apples, peeled and sliced
1/2 cup butter
1/2 cup flour
1 cup sugar
1/2 teaspoon salt
1/8 teaspoon nutmeg

Place sliced apples in a regular pie plate and sprinkle with nutmeg. Combine butter, flour, sugar and salt and mix together. Spread over top of the sliced apples. Bake at 350° F for 35 to 40 minutes until tender and brown.

Serves 6

If your tongue trips over "oolong"
and there's no place for your spoon,
If you end up with your cookie
on your knee,
If dainty conversation leaves you
speechless far too soon,
You need some help
surviving Ladies' Tea!

Haddyr Leigh

Ladies' Tea in the Sewing Room

Women in Portland's privileged class had surprisingly little free time. Their maids and cooks may have relieved them from the drudgery of housework and long hours over a hot stove, but they turned their attention to charitable causes, such as orphaned children and single mothers. Georgiana's circle of acquaintances met regularly to sew baby clothes and sip tea with their friends. A recipe or two might well have been shared during the busy afternoon.

Cream of Asparagus Soup

Asparagus season is short; this will help you make the most of it!

2 cups coarsely chopped asparagus (about 10 ounces)
1/2 cup coarsely chopped onion
1 cup water
1 chicken bouillon cube
1 teaspoon salt
1/8 teaspoon lemon pepper
2 1/2 cups milk
2 teaspoons cornstarch

In a 2-quart saucepan, place asparagus, onion, water, bouillon, salt and lemon pepper. Cover and simmer 25 minutes or until vegetables are very tender. In a medium bowl, gradually stir milk into cornstarch until smooth and add to saucepan, stirring constantly. Bring to a boil over medium heat and boil one minute, stirring constantly.

Serves 4

...ea is served! Delicious Orange Tea Balls make any tea a special occasion.

Meet the Ladies Sewing Circle from Portland's First Unitarian Church, whose good deeds improved the lot of the city's orphaned children. Georgiana Pittock was a long-time member. She is seated second from the right in the second row from the bottom.

Seafood Tart

Seafood was a favorite at Pittock Mansion.
Use crab, lobster or salmon in this delicious recipe.

2 beaten eggs
1/2 cup milk
2 Tablespoons flour
1/2 cup mayonnaise
1 2/3 cups flaked seafood, drained
1 8-ounce package Swiss cheese, shredded
1/3 cup sliced green onions
1 partially baked pie shell

Preheat oven to 350° F. Beat together the eggs and milk. Stir in the flour. Add the mayonnaise. Sprinkle seafood, cheese, and onion evenly in the partially baked pie shell. Pour egg mixture over all. Bake for 40 to 45 minutes or until knife inserted in center comes out clean.

Serves 6

Tester's Notes: This recipe is delicious and easy to make.

Strawberry Rhubarb Pie

A great recipe and a great way to enjoy two of our luscious summer edibles.

1 pound rhubarb, washed and trimmed
1 1/2 cups thickly sliced strawberries
1 1/2 cups sugar
1/2 to 2/3 cups flour, depending upon juiciness of berries
1/4 teaspoon each cloves and nutmeg
1 1/2 teaspoons cinnamon
Pastry for a double crust 9" pie
2 Tablespoons butter or margarine

Slice the rhubarb crosswise, 1/3" thick, to make about 3 cups. In a bowl, combine the rhubarb and the strawberries. Mix the sugar, flour, cloves, nutmeg and cinnamon and stir this into the fruit. Let stand about 15 minutes, stirring occasionally.

Preheat oven to 375° F. Roll a little more than half the pastry on a floured board to fit into a 9" pie pan so that the pastry extends about 1/2" beyond the rim.

Fill with fruit and dot with butter.

Roll out remaining pastry and cut in 1/2" wide strips. Weave the strips into a lattice for the upper crust. Bake on lowest shelf of oven for 35 to 40 minutes or until fruit bubbles and crust is well browned.

Serves 8

Tester's Notes: I put edge protectors on the rim of the pie to prevent over-browning. The pie had a delicious flavor and the spices were excellent.

Bouncing Babies

Yummy little treats that are a cross between a popover and a Dutch Baby.

2 cups flour (sift before measuring)
2 cups milk
2 Tablespoons powdered sugar
1 teaspoon salt
8 eggs

Preheat oven to 400° F. Place 2 cups milk in large bowl. Stir in sifted flour with an egg beater. Add the powdered sugar and salt, stirring well. Beat in 8 eggs, one at a time. Grease 12 custard cups. Pour in batter until custard cups are one-third full. Bake 20 minutes at 400° F, then lower to 350° F for 10 minutes or until done.

Serves 12

Tester's Notes: This makes a very large batch and could easily be cut in half. They received rave reviews from my sons who ate them with butter, powdered sugar, syrup, jam and/or ice cream.

The Waverly Home for orphaned children was a project that was dear
to Georgiana's heart.

This charming sewing table sits in the Sewing Room at Pittock Mansion.

Orange Tea Balls

This is a tasty version of a treat Henry Pittock II remembers
from his childhood. He called it "fried dough"!

Canola oil for deep frying

1 egg

1/2 cup milk

1 teaspoon vanilla

1 1/3 cups sifted flour

2 Tablespoons baking powder

1/4 teaspoon salt

1/3 cup sugar

2 teaspoons grated orange rind

1 Tablespoon melted shortening, cooled slightly

additional granulated or confectioner's sugar for dusting

Heat oil to 350° F. Beat egg. Add milk and vanilla, mixing well. Sift dry ingredients and add to egg and milk mixture, blending well. Stir in orange rind; do not beat. Stir in the one tablespoon of melted, cooled shortening. Drop a rounded teaspoonful of batter into the hot oil. Fry just a few at a time, about 3 to 5 minutes, turning the tea balls over when they come to the surface. Drain well on paper towels. Dust with sugar.

Serves: Makes 2 dozen tea balls

Tester's Notes: I used my "Fry Baby" and did not have to worry about the temperature.

Chocolate Fudge Upside Down Cake

Rich and chocolatey, it's a favorite with children and adults alike.

3/4 cup sugar
1 Tablespoon butter or margarine
1/2 cup milk
1 cup flour
1/4 teaspoon salt
1 teaspoon baking powder
1 1/2 Tablespoons unsweetened cocoa

Topping:
1/2 cup walnuts
1/2 cup sugar
1/2 cup brown sugar
1/4 cup cocoa
1 1/4 cups boiling water

Cream the 3/4 cup sugar, butter and milk together. Sift together the flour, salt, baking powder and 1 1/2 Tablespoons cocoa. Stir these mixtures together well. Spread in a 9-inch buttered pan and sprinkle with walnuts. After mixing, top with 1/2 cup sugar, 1/2 cup brown sugar and 1/4 cup cocoa. Pour boiling water over all and bake at 350° F for 30 minutes.

Orange Sour Cream Cookies

This is just a wonderful cookie—orangey and refreshing. It would be a nice touch to decorate the serving platter with either fresh or candied orange slices.

2 1/2 cups flour
1 teaspoon baking soda
1 1/2 cups brown sugar, packed
1/2 teaspoon salt
1/2 cup butter or margarine
2 eggs
1 teaspoon vanilla
1 teaspoon grated orange rind
1 cup dairy sour cream
1/2 cup chopped pecans

Sift dry ingredients and set aside. Cream butter or margarine and brown sugar. Add eggs, vanilla, orange rind and sour cream. Stir in dry ingredients, blending well. Add nuts. Drop by teaspoonfuls onto lightly greased cookie sheets. Bake at 350° F for 12 to 15 minutes. Top with frosting while still warm.

Frosting:
1 1/2 Tablespoons soft butter
1 1/2 teaspoons grated orange rind
3 Tablespoons orange juice
3 cups sifted powdered sugar

Combine all ingredients, beating until of spreading consistency. Spread about 1/4 teaspoon frosting on each warm cookie.

Makes: 5 dozen

"Charity begins at home."

Publius Terentius Afer

Fundraising Tea

Ten cents was the admission price to the Portland fundraising teas in Georgiana's day. Arrays of luscious cakes, pies, cookies and candy tempted visitors, who sat down to tea and who bought extra to take home for the family's dinner. These events, held at first in private homes and later in public facilities, not only raised significant funds for charitable causes, but were enjoyable social occasions.

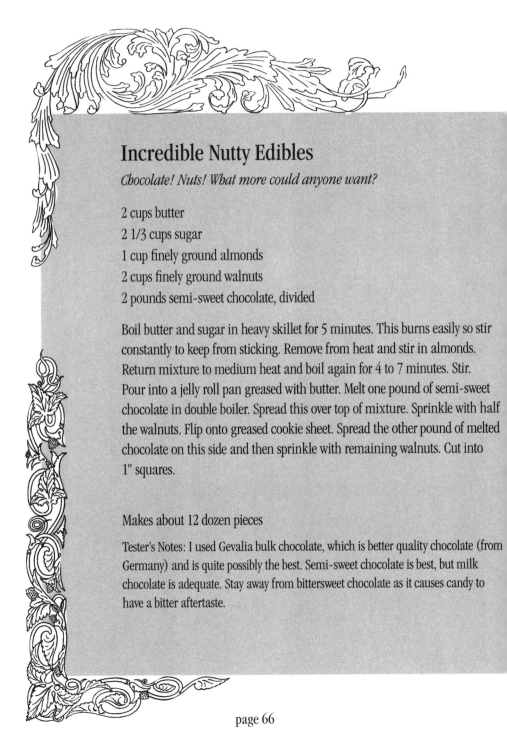

Incredible Nutty Edibles

Chocolate! Nuts! What more could anyone want?

2 cups butter
2 1/3 cups sugar
1 cup finely ground almonds
2 cups finely ground walnuts
2 pounds semi-sweet chocolate, divided

Boil butter and sugar in heavy skillet for 5 minutes. This burns easily so stir constantly to keep from sticking. Remove from heat and stir in almonds. Return mixture to medium heat and boil again for 4 to 7 minutes. Stir. Pour into a jelly roll pan greased with butter. Melt one pound of semi-sweet chocolate in double boiler. Spread this over top of mixture. Sprinkle with half the walnuts. Flip onto greased cookie sheet. Spread the other pound of melted chocolate on this side and then sprinkle with remaining walnuts. Cut into 1" squares.

Makes about 12 dozen pieces

Tester's Notes: I used Gevalia bulk chocolate, which is better quality chocolate (from Germany) and is quite possibly the best. Semi-sweet chocolate is best, but milk chocolate is adequate. Stay away from bittersweet chocolate as it causes candy to have a bitter aftertaste.

In the main hall at Pittock Mansion, a table-top display of goodies for a fundraising sale. Shown (*clockwise from right foreground*) Positively Perfect Pear Pie, No-fail Butter Mints, and wrapped packets of Almond Brittle

Hats of the era were often flights of fancy, with bows, flowers and feathers. Daughters Helen Louise ("Lucy") and Kate were decked out for tea in this c.1900 photograph.

Almond Brittle

Our tester said it well: "I can't tell you how many this would serve because I crave candy and could have eaten the whole thing. Yummy!"

2 cups whole blanched almonds
1 cup sugar
4 Tablespoons butter
1 teaspoon vanilla

In a heavy skillet, heat almonds, sugar and butter over medium heat. Stir constantly until almonds are toasted and sugar is golden, about 15 minutes. Stir in vanilla. Drop in clusters on baking sheet or foil or spread on marble. Cool.

Serves: Makes about 1 pound of candy

Positively Perfect Pear Pie

*Among the first trees to be planted at Pittock Mansion
were the apple and pear trees out near the "point".*

Pie Crust:

2 cups flour

1 teaspoon salt

2/3 cup shortening

5 to 6 Tablespoons ice water

Stir salt into flour with fork and fluff. Cut shortening into flour. Sprinkle ice
water over flour mixture. Stir quickly into ball. Roll out dough for a large pie
plate. Trim and crimp edges setting leftover crust aside for topping..

Filling:

6 to 7 large ripe Bartlett pears.

2 Tablespoons white vinegar

1/3 cup of flour

1 teaspoon allspice

Peel, core and cut pears in half, adding them to a bowl with water and
white vinegar. When finished, drain water and add flour and allspice. Mix
thoroughly but gently. Arrange pears in a pattern of concentric circles from
the outside in.

Topping:

Leftover piecrust
1/2 cup brown sugar
1/2 cup chopped walnuts
1/4 cup butter

With pastry cutter, cut leftover piecrust with brown sugar and butter. Stir in walnuts. Mix well and sprinkle over pears. Bake at 450° F for 20 to 30 minutes until crust is golden brown. Then lower heat to 350° F and bake 10 more minutes.

Serve warm with whipped cream or ice cream.

Candied Orange and Grapefruit Peel

*A tribute to Henry Pittock, who loved grapefruit so much, he even
made plans to build an orangerie, so that he could grow them
at Pittock Mansion.*

3 thick-skinned grapefruit
6 seedless oranges
Water
2 Tablespoons salt
Sugar

Wash fruit very well, then remove peel in quarter sections. Soak grapefruit
and orange peel overnight in 2 quarts of cold water to which the salt has been
added. Drain and place in a saucepan. Cover with cold water and bring to a
boil. Repeat this process three times, then cook until peel is soft. Drain and
cut with scissors into petal shaped pieces or diamond shapes. Weigh the peel;
put an equal weight of sugar into a saucepan and add a cup of water. Bring
syrup to boiling point, add the peel and cook gently until it is transparent and
tender. Remove each piece separately and put on rack to drain. When cool,
roll pieces in sugar and spread out on trays, one layer deep, to dry. Store in a
tightly covered container.

Serves: Makes about 8 dozen pieces

Tester's Notes: Serve this delicate sweet with vanilla ice cream desserts or pass it with
tea in place of a cookie.

Georgiana Pittock is shown here (*seated center*) at the 1917 opening celebration of the Washington Hotel, a residence for young women. This hotel, one of her pet projects, was established as a result of her fundraising efforts.

Carrot-Apple Cake

Carrots and apples were two of the fresh foods grown at Pittock Mansion. This is a hearty fall cake.

3/4 cup butter or margarine
1 cup granulated sugar
1 1/2 cups dark brown sugar
2 eggs
2 1/4 cups unsweetened applesauce
3 cups unsifted all-purpose flour
1 1/2 cups unsifted whole-wheat flour
3 teaspoons baking soda
1 1/2 teaspoons each cinnamon, nutmeg and allspice
3/4 cup shredded carrots
1 1/2 cups walnuts, chopped
1 1/2 cups raisins

Preheat oven to 350° F. Grease and flour a bundt cake pan. Cream together butter and sugars. Add eggs and mix well. Add applesauce alternately with dry ingredients, beating well between additions. When blended, fold in carrots, walnuts, and raisins.

Pour into prepared bundt pan and bake for 45 minutes and check. Cake is done when inserted toothpick comes out clean. Cool in pan 5 minutes and unmold.

Optional Cream Cheese Frosting

Mix together the following two ingredients, softened to room temperature:

1 8-ounce package cream cheese

1/2 cup butter or margarine

Add:

2 cups powdered sugar

If the frosting is too stiff, beat in a drop or two of either lemon juice or milk until spreading consistency is obtained.

Although not in the paid workforce, the women of Georgiana's circle worked hard to raise funds for social projects. Women and orphaned children were often the beneficiaries. Henry Pittock II can be seen in the background of this photo.

No-Fail Butter Mints

Such a pretty candy-almost too pretty to eat, but you will!

1/2 cup butter or margarine
1 Tablespoon water
1 pound powdered sugar
Few drops of peppermint flavoring or flavoring you like

Mix softened butter or margarine, water, and sifted powdered sugar in a sauce pan. Cook over low heat until smooth. Drop in little spots on wax paper or foil. Or roll into little patties.

Serves: Lots! Makes about 1 1/2 pounds of candy.

Tester's Notes: Almond flavoring is also good. If you use real butter instead of margarine, you will have a more buttery taste. Also, for today 's cooks, we have the option of using the candy molds which are available now.

Heavenly Hash Squares

*Chocolate lovers will be **so** happy with this one!*

4 slightly beaten eggs
2 cups sugar
1 cup butter or stick margarine, softened
4 Tablespoons cocoa, unsweetened
1 1/2 cups flour
2 cups chopped nuts or less
1 teaspoon vanilla
1 large (16-ounce) package mini marshmallows

Preheat oven to 325° F. Grease a 13 x 9-inch pan. In a large bowl, mix all ingredients together *except* marshmallows. Spoon into prepared pan and bake 40 minutes. Remove from oven and immediately sprinkle miniature marshmallows over top. Prepare icing.

Icing:

4 Tablespoons cocoa
1/2 cup melted butter or margarine
8 Tablespoons evaporated milk
1 16-ounce box powdered sugar

Heat cocoa, butter and milk until melted. Stir in powdered sugar. Pour icing over marshmallows. Refrigerate until icing hardens. When chilled, cut into squares and store in refrigerator.

Makes about 30 squares

Cherry Surprises

This is a cookie with a surprise inside. Good anytime of the year.
It's fun to watch your guests' faces as they bite into it!

1 cup butter, softened
Powdered sugar
1 teaspoon vanilla extract
1/2 cup finely chopped nuts
2 1/4 cups sifted cake flour
1 pound (about) candied cherries

Cream butter and 1/2 cup sugar until light and fluffy. Add flour and mix well.
Wrap dough in wax paper and chill well.
Then roll on lightly floured surface to 1/8 inch thickness. Cut round with
floured 1 3/4 inch cutter. Put a cherry in the center of each and shape into a
ball with lightly floured hands. Put on an ungreased cookie sheet and chill
15 minutes. Bake in 350° F oven for 15 minutes.
While still warm, roll in powdered sugar. Store in an airtight container
in a cool place.

Makes 7 dozen

Note: Substitute for cake flour: 1 cup minus 2 Tablespoons regular flour.

There are few hours in life more
agreeable than the hour dedicated
to the ceremony known as
afternoon tea.

Henry James

Afternoon Tea in the Music Room

The quintessential afternoon tea, served in the splendor of Pittock Mansion's oval drawing room, was an elegant affair. The Pittock daughters would often entertain guests, with Lucy playing the grand piano given to her by her father, and Kate singing in accompaniment.

Today, almost one hundred years later, that same piano is still in the Music Room and is played at Mansion events, with echoes of the early Pittock days.

Nanny's Yellow Sponge Cake

We have Bertha Pittock (alias "Nanny" to her grandchildren) to thank fo.
this classic recipe.

4 eggs, separated
1 cup granulated sugar
1 cup flour
1 teaspoon baking powder
1/2 teaspoon salt
1/2 cup orange juice

Preheat oven to 350° F. Line the bottom of two 8-inch ungreased layer pans
with a circle of parchment paper or waxed paper. (It's important that the
pans not be greased.) In a medium mixing bowl, beat the 4 egg whites until
stiff peaks are formed. Set aside. In a large mixing bowl, beat the 4 egg yolks.
Add the sugar and mix well. Add the orange juice and beat until well blended.
Add the sifted flour mixture and beat until blended. With a spatula, gently
fold in the beaten egg whites.

Pour into the prepared pans. Bake for 25 to 30 minutes or until done. Serve
with fresh fruit such as sliced strawberries or peaches and whipped cream. Or
use sponge cake rounds in the Ambrosia Cake recipe which follows.

Afternoon tea awaits guests in Pittock's oval Music Room.
Scrumptious Cherry Angel Roll is on the menu, shown here
in front of the original 1887 Steinway grand piano that
Henry purchased for daughter Lucy.

Susan Pittock, daughter of Henry and Georgiana,
wore her lovely lace-trimmed gown for this
photograph, taken around 1900. The gown
is now a treasured item in the Pittcock
Mansion Society Collection.

Ambrosia Cake

A lovely use for Nanny's Yellow Sponge Cake.

2 sponge cake rounds—see Nanny's Yellow Sponge Cake recipe, p. 82
3 cups sweetened whipped cream (divided)
3 or 4 navel oranges, sliced 1/2 inch thick
Berry jelly

Spread one cake layer with one third of the whipped cream.
Top with one third of the coconut and half of the orange slices.
Place the second cake layer on top; repeat cream, coconut, and orange toppings.
Fill centers of orange slices with jelly. Frost sides of cake with the remaining
third of whipped cream and coconut. Refrigerate until serving time.

Serves 8 to 10

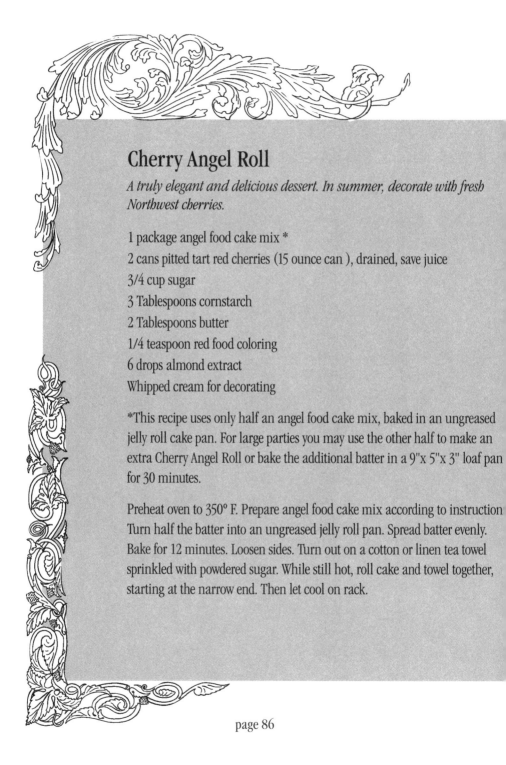

Cherry Angel Roll

A truly elegant and delicious dessert. In summer, decorate with fresh Northwest cherries.

1 package angel food cake mix *
2 cans pitted tart red cherries (15 ounce can), drained, save juice
3/4 cup sugar
3 Tablespoons cornstarch
2 Tablespoons butter
1/4 teaspoon red food coloring
6 drops almond extract
Whipped cream for decorating

*This recipe uses only half an angel food cake mix, baked in an ungreased jelly roll cake pan. For large parties you may use the other half to make an extra Cherry Angel Roll or bake the additional batter in a 9"x 5"x 3" loaf pan for 30 minutes.

Preheat oven to 350° F. Prepare angel food cake mix according to instruction Turn half the batter into an ungreased jelly roll pan. Spread batter evenly. Bake for 12 minutes. Loosen sides. Turn out on a cotton or linen tea towel sprinkled with powdered sugar. While still hot, roll cake and towel together, starting at the narrow end. Then let cool on rack.

Meanwhile, drain the cherries, reserving 3/4 cup juice—set aside a few whole cherries for garnish. In a small bowl, combine sugar, cornstarch, and a dash of salt. In a saucepan, heat the reserved cherry juice to boiling and gradually stir this into the sugar mixture. Return to the saucepan. Cook and stir until thickened and clear. Stir in butter, almond extract and cherries. Cool. Unroll cake and spread with filling. Roll up, placing seam down. Trim with whipped cream or dust with powdered sugar and decorate with cherries. When in season, fresh cherries may be used as decoration..

Tester's Notes: The second time I made this, I used a canned cherry pie filling, but adding the butter and the almond extract. This was an improvement, because it gave a nicer (redder) look to the finished dessert. Two cans of cherry pie filling would give you a nice, generous filling.

Editor's Comments: We have not included any recipes that called for ingredients which were not available to the Pittocks. However, we made an exception in this case. Angel Food Cake mix was not available to them, but this recipe sounded so very good, we decided to include it. Obviously, if you wish to make the cake from scratch you may do so.

Serves 10

Pineapple Pecan Bread

A moist bread that also makes a delicious breakfast bread when toasted.

3/4 cup brown sugar
1/4 cup shortening
1 egg
2 cups sifted flour
1 teaspoon baking soda
1/2 teaspoon salt
1/3 cup orange juice concentrate, thawed (half a 6-ounce can)
1 cup crushed pineapple, undrained (1 8 1/4-ounce can)
1/2 cup chopped pecans

Preheat oven to 350° F. Grease 9"x5"x3" loaf pan. Cream together brown sugar and shortening. Add egg and mix well. Sift together dry ingredients and add t sugar mixture. Blend in orange juice concentrate, then add pineapple. Fold in pecans.

Spoon into prepared pan. Bake until bread tests dry in center and top is golden brown, about 50 to 60 minutes.

Cool on wire rack. Makes one loaf.

Lucy Pittock Gantenbein is ready for an elegant occasion
in this frothy dress.

Dressed and ready for afternoon tea are Georgiana Pittock's niece and nepl
Charles Gallien and Louise Gallien Barry, with their Aunty VanHouten (*in*

Lace Cookies

A crunchy delight. Bet you can't eat just one!

2 beaten eggs
1 cup packed brown sugar
1 heaping Tablespoon of flour
1 cup chopped nuts

In a medium mixing bowl, beat eggs till frothy. Blend in brown sugar. Stir in flour and chopped nuts mixing thoroughly. Drop by teaspoonfuls onto a cookie sheet lined with parchment paper. Bake at 375° F for 8 to 10 minutes on top rack of oven. Let cookies set for a few minutes before removing them to cool on a wire rack.

Makes 2 dozen

Toasted Coconut Pie

This will surely become your favorite coconut pie recipe. The toasted coconut makes it especially good.

3 eggs
1 1/2 cups sugar
1/2 cup melted butter or margarine
4 teaspoons lemon juice
1 teaspoon vanilla
1 cup flaked coconut
1 unbaked 9-inch pastry shell

Preheat oven to 350° F. Beat eggs well. Add sugar, butter, lemon juice and vanilla. Stir in coconut. Pour into unbaked pastry shell. Bake for about one hour or until knife inserted comes out clean. Cool before serving. Top with whipped cream and toasted coconut, if you like.

Serves 8

Tester's Notes: Different and simply great!

Nicely Icy Party Punch

This is a very refreshing punch—light, fruity, and would also be wonderful served at a garden party.

6 cups water

4 cups sugar

1 (12-ounce) can frozen orange juice

2 fresh lemons

5 ripe bananas

1 (46-ounce) can pineapple juice

3 (28-ounce) bottles ginger ale, chilled

Heat water and sugar to dissolve. Dilute orange juice as directed.

Blend bananas in blender with a little sugar water, and lemons quartered and seeded. Mix all ingredients well.

Cool and freeze in two containers (ice cream or plastic cartons or ring molds). Place in punch bowl about 3 hours before serving.

Add the ginger ale just before the party.

Serves 50

There is a great deal of poetry and
fine sentiment in a chest of tea.

Ralph Waldo Emerson

High Tea in the Dining Room

"High Tea", often considered a "working man's tea," was hearty and delicious. Today it would be the equivalent of our "light supper" and would include dishes that were both savory and sweet.

Our high tea recipes feature foods that were favorites of the Pittocks. Seafood was often served at the Mansion, as was chicken, from the poultry farm owned by Henry, along with vegetables and fruits from the Mansion gardens.

Dungeness Crab Bisque

At the turn of the century, seafood was a popular item on Portland menus. Fresh Northwest crabmeat, rather than imitation crab, is essential for this wonderful recipe.

1 pound fresh crab

2 Tablespoons butter

1/4 cup roasted red pepper or pimiento, finely sliced

1/2 pound mushrooms, sliced

3 stalks celery, chopped

1/2 onion, finely chopped

2 medium shallots, finely chopped

2 cups milk

1/2 cup cream

1 cup white wine, a good quality Sauterne

2 chicken bouillon cubes

1/2 teaspoon paprika

1/2 teaspoon nutmeg

Salt and pepper to taste

Several drops of Tabasco, to taste

Croutons for garnish, optional.

Lightly sauté mushrooms, celery, onion and shallots in butter in large soup kettle. Add roasted red pepper, wine, milk, cream, chicken bouillon cubes and crab. Let the bisque cook gently over low heat, stirring to avoid burning. Add more milk if a thinner soup is desired. Do not allow to boil. Garnish with croutons.

If this soup will be reheated, add crabmeat just before serving.

Henry and Georgiana's son, Fred Francis Pittock, and his wife,
Bertha, affectionately known as "Bird", stand on the steps
of their Portland home.

PHOTO BY MICHAEL HENLEY, CONTEMPORARY IMAGES.

Sticky Toffee Pudding, a recipe that points to Henry's British roots,
is shown in the Pittock Mansion dining room, ready to serve at High Tea.

Puget Sound Oyster Stew

Another excellent seafood recipe, surely a favorite with the family.

4 Tablespoons butter

1 large onion, chopped

1/2 cup lightly packed, fresh parsley, or 2 Tablespoons dried parsley flakes

1 large green pepper, seeded and chopped (optional)

2 14-ounce cans chicken broth

1 cup dry white wine

2 medium potatoes, peeled and cut in 1/2-inch cubes

1/2 to 1 cup whipping cream

2 to 3 cups raw oysters and juices, cutting large oysters bite size

Melt butter in at least a 4 quart size kettle. Add onion, parsley and green pepper (if desired). Cook, stirring until onion is soft. Add chicken broth and white wine. Cover and bring to boil. Add potatoes and simmer 10 to 15 minutes or until potatoes are tender. Add whipping cream and oysters. Simmer 1 to 2 minutes longer, or until hot. Ladle into bowls to serve.

Serves 4 to 6

Chicken Divine

*Chicken was always popular at the Mansion and was served
roasted every Sunday.*

4 skinless, boned, chicken breast halves

2 Tablespoons flour combined with 1/2 teaspoon salt and dash of pepper

2 Tablespoons vegetable oil

2 Tablespoons flour

1/2 cup chicken broth

1/2 cup milk

1/4 teaspoon dried tarragon, crumbled (optional)

3 cups broccoli florets, cooked until tender-crisp

2 Tablespoons bread crumbs

Coat chicken with seasoned flour. Brown in hot oil. Reduce heat to low,
cover and cook 15-20 minutes or until done. Remove chicken to baking dish.
Top with cooked broccoli florets. Set aside. Save pan with drippings. Stir in
2 Tablespoons flour. Add broth, milk, salt and pepper to taste and tarragon
if desired. Cook about 2 minutes or until thickened. Pour sauce over chicken
and broccoli. Sprinkle with bread crumbs. Brown under broiler.

Serves 4

Spinach Soufflé

Even those who say they won't eat spinach will love this. Light and tasty!

3 Tablespoons butter
3 Tablespoons flour
1 cup milk
1 cup chopped spinach, cooked and well-drained
2 Tablespoons minced onion
6 egg yolks, beaten
6 egg whites, stiffly beaten

Melt butter; add flour and blend. Stir in milk and cook until sauce thickens. Season with salt and pepper to taste. Add spinach and onion. Cool and add well beaten egg yolks. Fold in stiffly beaten egg whites. Put in an ungreased baking dish. Bake at 325° F for about 45 minutes.

Serves 4

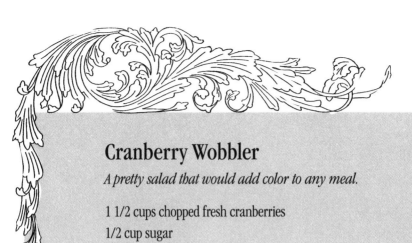

Cranberry Wobbler

A pretty salad that would add color to any meal.

1 1/2 cups chopped fresh cranberries
1/2 cup sugar
1/4 teaspoon salt
1/4 teaspoon cinnamon
1/8 teaspoon cloves
2 3-oz. packages (or 1 6-oz. package) Jello, orange or lemon flavor
2 cups boiling water
1 1/2 cups cold water
1 Tablespoon lemon juice
1 orange, peeled, sectioned and diced
1/2 cup chopped almonds or walnuts

Combine cranberries, sugar, salt, cinnamon and cloves in a small bowl; set aside. In a large mixing bowl, combine Jello and boiling water. Stir until gelatin is dissolved. Add cold water and lemon juice, stirring well. Refrigerate jello mixture until it thickens slightly. Add cranberry mixture, orange pieces and nuts. Stir to combine. Pour into a large 6-cup mold (or bowl).

Refrigerate approximately 4 hours or until firm. Just before serving, unmold salad on a decorative plate. To unmold easily, run the point of a knife around edge of gelatin, dip mold in a basin of hot water for just one second, cover top with plate and invert.

Makes 6 cups or 12 servings

Tester's notes: "This salad has a beautiful color! A can of drained mandarin oranges can be substituted for a fresh orange. This recipe easily serves 12."

Sticky Toffee Pudding

Sticky Toffee Pudding is an old English tradition. Since Henry Pittock was born in Britain, we think the family probably enjoyed this pudding very much. It is truly yummy.

1/4 cup butter or margarine
3/4 cup granulated sugar
1 cup flour
1 teaspoon baking powder
1 egg
3/4 cup pitted dates, chopped
1 cup boiling water
1 teaspoon baking soda
1 teaspoon vanilla

Toffee Sauce

1/2 cup butter
3/4 cup brown sugar
1/4 cup cream or half-and-half

Preheat oven to 350° F. Grease a 9" square cake pan. In a small mixing bowl, pour the boiling water over the dates and soda and set aside. In a large mixing bowl, cream the butter and sugar together until pale in color. Gradually stir in the egg, flour and baking powder. Mix well. Stir in the dates with the liquid and then the vanilla. Pour into the prepared pan and bake for 40 minutes until firm to the touch.

To make the sauce, combine all ingredients in a medium saucepan. Bring to a boil, stirring constantly. Continue to boil for 2 minutes. Remove from heat. Just before serving, pour the sauce over the warm pudding after it has been cut and placed in bowls.

Portland Pear Cake

We couldn't resist including this recipe, since we know the Pittocks loved pears, and our Pacific Northwest pears are SO good!

3 cups flour

2 cups sugar

1/2 teaspoon cinnamon

1 1/2 teaspoons baking soda

1/2 teaspoon nutmeg

1 teaspoon salt

3 eggs

1 1/2 cups cooking oil

1 teaspoon vanilla

3 cups finely peeled and chopped pears

Pecans or walnuts optional

Sift dry ingredients together. Mix these ingredients well. Beat 3 eggs and add the oil, vanilla, pears and nuts.

Pour mixture into a greased and floured bundt pan and bake at 350 degrees for 1 hour and 15 minutes. Or, pour mixture into 2 loaf pans and bake for approximately 1 hour.

You may decorate the top of the cake with candied cherries for a more festive look.

Serves 20 to 25

What is the magic of tea?
As festive as Christmas pudding
Or as homey as fresh-baked buns.
A pick-me-up or a soothe-me-down,
Fence-mender, unwinder,
Justice of the Peace.
Regal, raucous, coy or solemn,
Tea speaks a language we all
understand.

S. H. Dow

Christmas Tea in the Library

Pittock Mansion is lovely in any season, but at Christmas, it glows! In the early Pittock days, the decorated Mansion was filled with the scents of fresh fir and cedar garland, twined with cut holly from the grounds. A tall tree graced the main hall near the stairway and presents for the family magically appeared under its lower branches.

Here's a splendid Christmas tea, to be served in the library.

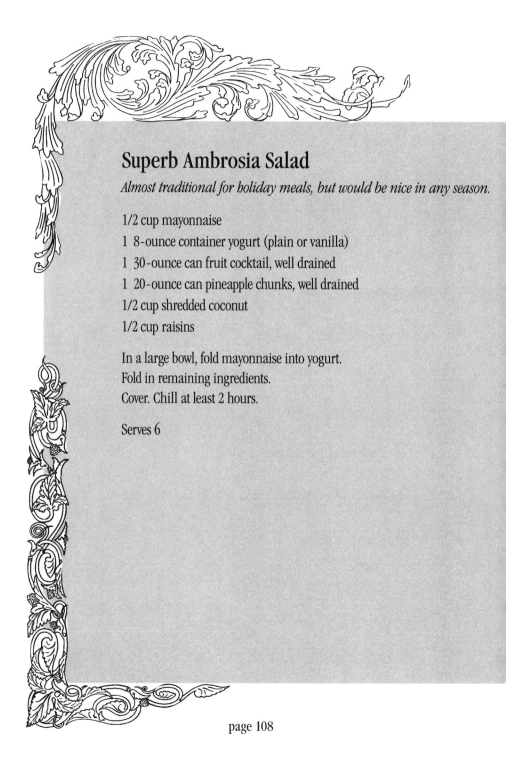

Superb Ambrosia Salad

Almost traditional for holiday meals, but would be nice in any season.

1/2 cup mayonnaise
1 8-ounce container yogurt (plain or vanilla)
1 30-ounce can fruit cocktail, well drained
1 20-ounce can pineapple chunks, well drained
1/2 cup shredded coconut
1/2 cup raisins

In a large bowl, fold mayonnaise into yogurt.
Fold in remaining ingredients.
Cover. Chill at least 2 hours.

Serves 6

Mrs. Virginia Pittock Thorsen shown with her children (*left to right*),
Warren Jr. and Fred, beside a Christmas nativity scene.

A group of Henry and Georgiana's descendants, the family of Fred and Bertha Pittock, posed for a group photograph one Christmas (c. 1930's)

British Shortbread Cookies

These delicate, buttery cookies seem to melt in your mouth!

1 cup butter
2 cups flour, divided, plus more as needed
1/3 cup brown sugar
Red or green glacé cherries for decoration, optional

In mixing bowl, cream butter. Add sugar and cream well until slightly fluffy. Mix in one cup of flour until a soft, easily handled dough is formed.

Flour a flat surface suitable for rolling dough. Turn dough out onto the floured surface and knead in some of the remaining flour gradually, until small cracks begin to show at edge of dough when it is pressed. (You may not need all of the flour. Too much flour will produce cookies that are tough and tasteless.) Wrap and chill dough one hour for easier handling.

Preheat oven to 325° F. Roll dough to 1/4" thickness. Cut into 1" x 2" strips or use a small cookie cutter. Strips can be pricked lightly with a fork three times for decoration, or each cookie can be decorated with half a glacé cherry, if desired. Bake for 12 to 15 minutes until a light golden color.

Makes about 4 dozen cookies

Pittock Pound Cake Tea Sandwiches

A lovely way to serve pound cake.

9 eggs, separated

1/2 teaspoon salt

1/2 teaspoon cream of tartar

2 cups granulated sugar

2 cups butter

1 teaspoon grated mace or nutmeg

1 1/2 teaspoons vanilla

3 Tablespoons brandy (or 1/4 teaspoon brandy extract)

4 cups sifted cake flour (or 3 1/2 cups sifted all-purpose flour)

Tea Sandwich filling:

fruit-flavored cream cheese

Preheat oven to 375° F. Grease and flour a bundt pan or two 5"x 9" loaf pans.

In a large mixing bowl, beat the egg whites with an electric mixer until stiff, adding salt and cream of tartar. Add sugar gradually, beating until a stiff meringue is formed.

In a second large bowl, whip butter until very soft; add egg yolks one at a time, continuing to beat. Add nutmeg, vanilla and brandy. Add flour slowly, beating well after each addition; this will form a very stiff, dough-like batter. Add about one third of the meringue and whip together. Gently fold in remaining meringue. Pour into the prepared pan(s) and bake until done,approximately 1 hour and 15 minutes for the Bundt pan or 1 hour for the loaf pans. Cool in the pan(s) for 15 minutes, then turn out onto a wire rack.

When cake is cool (preferably the next day), slice thin and sandwich together with a fruit-flavored cream cheese filling. Use a small decorative cutter to cut sandwiches into pretty tea party shapes.

Tester's notes: "The unique process of folding in a meringue vs. the more common process of folding in beaten egg whites helps significantly to hold volume and results in a very even texture. The result is a very fine-grade cake that was flavorful by itself, and makes excellent shortcake or delicate tea sandwiches."

Peppermint Candy Cookies

This is a pretty and tasty cookie, which would be very festive served at Christmas.

Dough:

1 cup (2 sticks) sweet unsalted butter

1/2 cup confectioner's sugar

2 1/2 cups unsifted all-purpose flour

1/2 cup chopped nuts

1 teaspoon vanilla

Filling:

1/2 cup crushed peppermint candy

1/2 cup confectioner's sugar

2 Tablespoons cream cheese

1 teaspoon milk

1 drop red food coloring

Dough: Cream butter with the sugar. Gradually add flour, nuts and vanilla. Mix thoroughly. Chill.

Filling: Combine candy and sugar. Reserve about one fourth for topping cookie. Blend cream cheese and milk and add to remaining candy mixture. Add food coloring. Mix well. Remove dough from refrigerator. Preheat oven to 350° F. Shape into balls about 1-inch in diameter. Make a deep hole with your finger in center of each ball and fill with about 1/4 teaspoon of filling. Seal with a small bit of dough. Place on ungreased cookie sheet and bake for about 10 minutes until set but not brown. Cool slightly on wire racks. While cookies are still warm, sprinkle with reserved candy mixture.

A splendid Pumpkin Rum Cake awaits Christmas tea in the library.

Pumpkin Eggnog Pie

Pumpkin and eggnog-it must be Christmas. Great pie, great crust!

Pie crust:

1 cup graham cracker crumbs

1/2 cup ground filberts

3 Tablespoons granulated sugar

6 Tablespoons butter, melted

Pie filling:

1 envelope unflavored gelatin

1/2 cup brown sugar

1 1/4 cups canned pumpkin

3 egg yolks

1 cup dairy eggnog

1 cup whipping cream

3 Tablespoons powdered sugar

1/4 teaspoon salt

1/2 teaspoon cinnamon

1/2 teaspoon nutmeg

1/2 teaspoon ginger

1/2 teaspoon allspice

1/4 teaspoon rum flavoring

Additional whipped cream as a garnish if desired

In a small bowl, combine graham cracker crumbs, ground filberts, sugar and melted butter. Stir together then press firmly into a 9" pie plate. Bake at 375° F for 6 to 8 minutes or until edges of crust are golden brown. Remove from oven and cool.

In a saucepan combine the unflavored gelatin, brown sugar, salt, cinnamon, nutmeg, ginger and allspice. Stir in eggnog, egg yolks, and pumpkin. Cook and stir over medium heat until gelatin dissolves and mixture thickens slightly. Remove from heat and chill until partly set. Meanwhile, whip cream until soft peaks form. Blend in powdered sugar. Fold whipped cream into pumpkin mixture. Spoon into crust. Chill until firm, about 4 hours. Garnish with additional whipped cream if desired.

A repousse silver tea and coffee service was a gift to Pittock Mansion.

Pumpkin Rum Cake

The combination of pumpkin and rum gives an aroma that's impossible to resist.

1 cup butter

2 cups sugar

4 eggs

1 1/2 cups canned pumpkin

2 Tablespoons rum (or 1 teaspoon rum flavoring + 1 Tablespoon milk)

3 1/4 cup flour, unsifted

3 teaspoons baking powder

1/2 teaspoon salt

2 teaspoons cinnamon

3/4 teaspoon each: ginger and nutmeg

1/2 teaspoon cloves

Whipped Rum Topping:

1 cup (1/2 pint) heavy whipping cream

2 Tablespoons powdered sugar

1/8 teaspoon nutmeg

1 Tablespoon rum (or 1/4 teaspoon rum flavoring)

Preheat oven to 350° F. Grease and flour a Bundt pan. Sift together flour, baking powder, salt, cinnamon, ginger, nutmeg and cloves. Set aside.

In a large mixing bowl, cream butter and sugar until fluffy. Add eggs and blend well, then add pumpkin and rum (or rum flavoring and milk). Stir well. Gradually blend in flour, mixing well after each addition. Pour into the greased and floured Bundt pan and bake at 350° F for 55 minutes or until done. Cool in pan 15 minutes, then invert on to a plate.

To prepare topping, whip cream with an electric mixer in a small bowl until fluffy soft peaks form. Sprinkle in powdered sugar, nutmeg and rum (or rum flavoring). Continue beating until stiff. Serve with slices of the cake.

Tester's notes: "This is a yummy cake with a pumpkin pie flavor! Originally it was baked in a tube pan, but it makes a lovely presentation when baked in a Bundt pan."

Frosty Fruitcake

This is a truly beautiful frosted white fruitcake that will look so elegant on a cake stand at your Christmas party or open house. Even non-fruitcake-lovers like this one.

3 cups chopped mixed candied fruits (your choice)
1 cup golden raisins
1 cup chopped, blanched almonds or almond slices
2 3/4 cups sifted flour
1 cup butter or margarine
1 cup sugar
1/4 teaspoon salt
4 eggs
1/4 cup light corn syrup
1/2 cup orange juice

Frosting:

1/4 cup corn syrup
3/4 cup granulated sugar
2 egg whites
2 Tablespoons water
A pinch of salt
1/4 teaspoon cream of tartar
1 teaspoon lemon or vanilla extract
Tiny candy canes (optional) for decoration

Preheat oven to 275° F. Grease a standard Bundt pan. Combine the fruits and nuts; toss lightly with 3/4 cup of the flour and set aside.

Cream together the butter, sugar and salt until light and fluffy. Add the eggs, one at a time, beating well after each addition until light and fluffy. Combine the corn syrup and the orange juice; add to creamed mixture alternately with remaining 2 cups of flour. Fold in the floured fruits and nuts.

Turn batter into prepared pan. Bake in very slow oven (275° F) for 2 hours or until cake tester inserted in center comes out clean. Cool cake in pan. Loosen around edges with knife and turn out on cake plate.

To prepare frosting, in top portion of a double boiler (over boiling water in the lower), place corn syrup, sugar, egg whites, water, salt and cream of tartar. Cook, beating constantly with an electric mixer or rotary hand mixer until soft peaks are formed when mixer is lifted. Be sure to keep the water in the lower portion at boiling temperature. Remove from heat, stir in extract, and continue to beat until sturdy peaks are formed and frosting is at a spreading consistency.

Frost cake immediately and decorate with tiny candy canes.

Serves 24

In 1939, Peggy Janet Victors married Henry Pittock II. From that time on, she put together a collection of recipes from her family and friends—the collection that inspired this cookbook. Shown here, in a photograph that was Peggy favorite, are the happy young couple on their honeymoon. We wish that Peggy had lived to see the book in print, but sadly she passed away on March 21, 200 She is deeply missed by those who knew this kind and gracious woman. .

Acknowledgments

This book is dedicated to all of the Pittock cooks, past and present. The inspiration for *Afternoon Tea at Pittock Mansion* came from a treasure trove of recipes gathered by the late Peggy Victors Pittock, wife of Henry Pittock II. (Henry is the grandson of Henry and Georgiana Pittock who built Pittock Mansion.)

Pittock family historian Janet Wilson brought Peggy's recipes to the attention of the Board of Directors of the Pittock Mansion Society. Gradually a book evolved, incorporating recipes, old photographs and fascinating bits of history, but unfortunately Peggy Pittock did not live to see the completion of this work.

The production of *Afternoon Tea at Pittock Mansion* has been made possible by the devoted efforts of many people who have so willingly offered their talents and time. The work of the Cookbook Committee, ably chaired by Barbara Scholl, is greatly appreciated. Other members of the committee included Heather Kibbey (editor/writer), Janet Wilson (historical data), Sueanne Townley (pen and ink drawings) and Diane Gronholm & Nancy Burns (our recipe accuracy team).

Invaluable also was the help of Pittock Mansion Director Daniel Crandall and Curator Lucy McLean Smith, who opened the archives and assisted in photo selection. Henry Pittock II graciously helped with photo identification. Michael Henley, of Contemporary Images, is to be congratulated for his photography on the back cover and throughout the book.

Thank you also to Janora Bayot, for her lovely cover illustration; Robert Selby of Design Studio Selby, for outstanding graphic design and prepress work; and Bob Smith of BookPrinters' Network who, along with United Graphics, was responsible for speeding the project through the printing process.

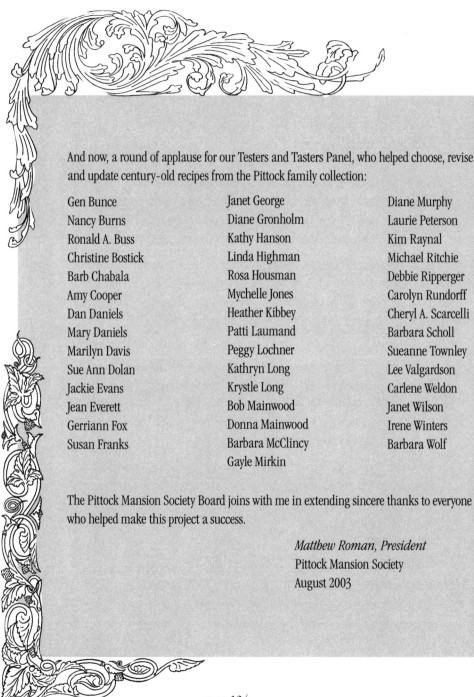

And now, a round of applause for our Testers and Tasters Panel, who helped choose, revise and update century-old recipes from the Pittock family collection:

Gen Bunce	Janet George	Diane Murphy
Nancy Burns	Diane Gronholm	Laurie Peterson
Ronald A. Buss	Kathy Hanson	Kim Raynal
Christine Bostick	Linda Highman	Michael Ritchie
Barb Chabala	Rosa Housman	Debbie Ripperger
Amy Cooper	Mychelle Jones	Carolyn Rundorff
Dan Daniels	Heather Kibbey	Cheryl A. Scarcelli
Mary Daniels	Patti Laumand	Barbara Scholl
Marilyn Davis	Peggy Lochner	Sueanne Townley
Sue Ann Dolan	Kathryn Long	Lee Valgardson
Jackie Evans	Krystle Long	Carlene Weldon
Jean Everett	Bob Mainwood	Janet Wilson
Gerriann Fox	Donna Mainwood	Irene Winters
Susan Franks	Barbara McClincy	Barbara Wolf
	Gayle Mirkin	

The Pittock Mansion Society Board joins with me in extending sincere thanks to everyone who helped make this project a success.

Matthew Roman, President
Pittock Mansion Society
August 2003

INDEX

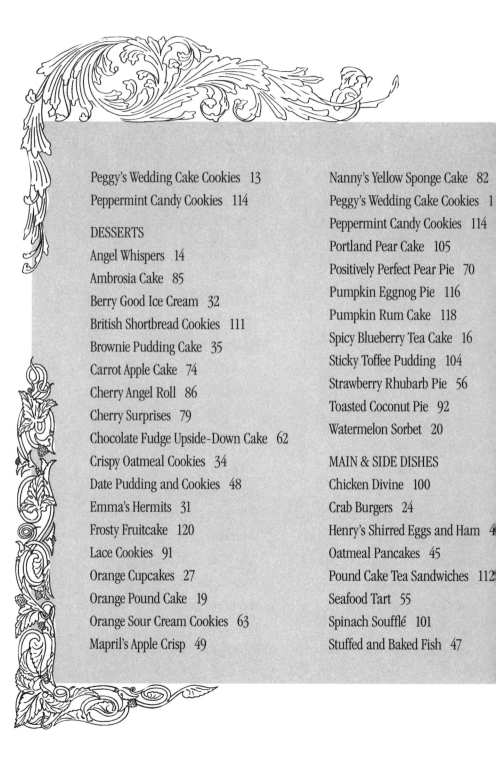

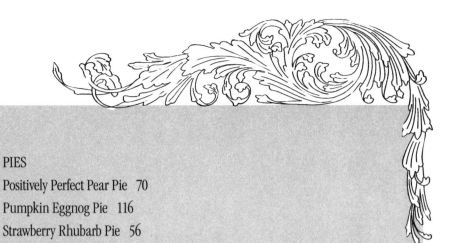

PIES

Positively Perfect Pear Pie   70
Pumpkin Eggnog Pie   116
Strawberry Rhubarb Pie   56
Toasted Coconut Pie   92

PUDDINGS

Brownie Pudding Cake   35
Date Pudding and Cookies   48
Sticky Toffee Pudding   104

SALADS

Cranberry Wobbler   102
Superb Ambrosia Salad   108

SOUPS

Chinese Chicken Mushroom Soup   38
Cream of Asparagus Soup   52
Dungeness Crab Bisque   96
Fresh Tomato Soup   41
Puget Sound Oyster Stew   99

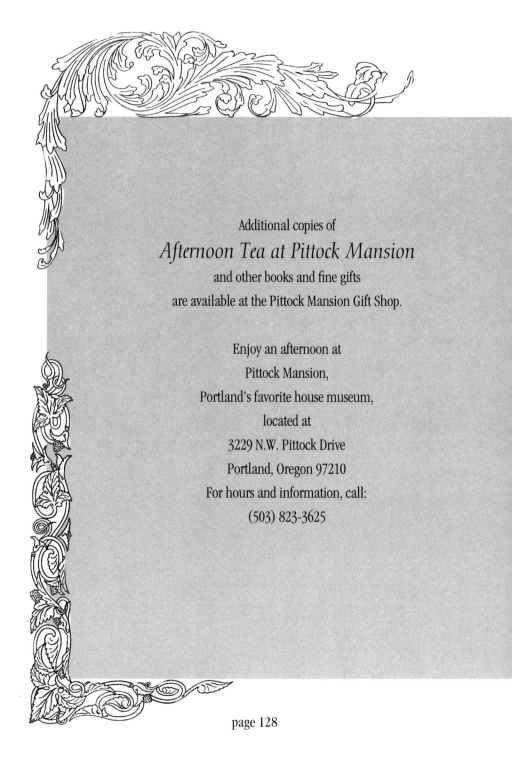

Additional copies of

Afternoon Tea at Pittock Mansion

and other books and fine gifts
are available at the Pittock Mansion Gift Shop.

Enjoy an afternoon at
Pittock Mansion,
Portland's favorite house museum,
located at
3229 N.W. Pittock Drive
Portland, Oregon 97210
For hours and information, call:
(503) 823-3625